ULTIMATE PUZZLE CHALLENGE

BRAIN SIZZLERS

By
Helene Hovanec

Illustrated by
Matt Luxich

STERLING

New York / London
www.sterlingpublishing.com/kids

STERLING and the distinctive Sterling logo are registered trademarks of
Sterling Publishing Co., Inc.

Lot # : 10 9 8 7 6 5 4 3 2 1
.11/09
Published by Sterling Publishing Co., Inc.
387 Park Avenue South, New York, NY 10016
© 2009 by Helene Hovanec
Illustrations © 2009 by Matt Luxich
Distributed in Canada by Sterling Publishing
℅ Canadian Manda Group, 165 Dufferin Street
Toronto, Ontario, Canada M6K 3H6
Distributed in the United Kingdom by GMC Distribution Services
Castle Place, 166 High Street, Lewes, East Sussex, England BN7 1XU
Distributed in Australia by Capricorn Link (Australia) Pty. Ltd.
P.O. Box 704, Windsor, NSW 2756, Australia

Sterling ISBN 978-1-4027-6203-1

For information about custom editions, special sales, premium and
corporate purchases, please contact Sterling Special Sales
Department at 800-805-5489 or specialsales@sterlingpublishing.com.

INTRODUCTION

Welcome to the **Ultimate Puzzle Challenge**—a brand new series of books for children who love word searches, crisscrosses, mazes, crosswords, and variety puzzles. As an added bonus, many puzzles are based on silly riddles that will make you giggle or smile.

I hope that **Brain Sizzlers** will amuse and challenge you at the same time. You may whiz through some puzzles in just a few minutes, but others might make your brain work overtime. There are no rules to follow except the directions before each puzzle, so go through the book at your own pace. If you don't know something, it's okay to ask for help, use a dictionary, or even peek at the answer—these are all good ways to learn! The main goal is to have fun and exercise your brain.

Take the **Ultimate Puzzle Challenge** . . . and enjoy!

—Helene Hovanec

EASY AS PIE

Take time to smell the bakery aromas as you sift through the picture to find and circle the names of the eight bakery products listed below.

Bread	Cookies	Doughnut	Pie
Cake	Cupcake	Muffin	Roll

Answers on page 85.

MAGIC SQUARES

In a magic square, the answer words are the same both **ACROSS** and **DOWN**. So, answer each clue with a four-letter word and put it in the grid both ways. We did the first one for you.

1. Unlock
2. Section of glass
3. Finishes
4. Bird's home

	1	2	3	4
1	O	P	E	N
2	P	a	n	e
3	E	n	d	s
4	N	e	s	t

A

1. Take with force
2. Heavy cord
3. Monkeys
4. Opposite of worst

	1	2	3	4
1				
2				
3				
4				

B

1. Spinning toys
2. The shape of an egg
3. Mama's husband
4. Hit hard

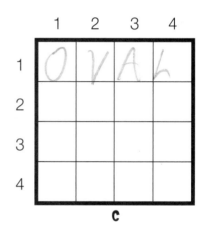

C

1. "___ White and the Seven Dwarfs"
2. Number of players on a baseball team
3. A single time only
4. An unwanted plant

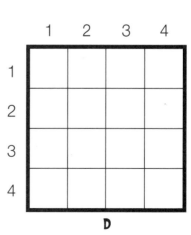

D

Answers on page 86.

SUM SITUATION

Use this code to find a riddle and its answer.

A = 26	N = 13
B = 25	O = 12
C = 24	P = 11
D = 23	Q = 10
E = 22	R = 9
F = 21	S = 8
G = 20	T = 7
H = 19	U = 6
I = 18	V = 5
J = 17	W = 4
K = 16	X = 3
L = 15	Y = 2
M = 14	Z = 1

4 19 26 7   23 18 23   12 13 22

What DID one

14 26 7 19   25 12 12 16 8 26 2 7 12

mats Book SAy to

7 19 22   12 7 19 22 9   14 26 7 19

the other mat

25 12 12 16 ?   25 12 2 ,   23 12   18

BooK? Boy Do I

19 26 5 22   11 9 12 25 15 22 14 8 .

have ProBLems

Answers on page 92.

MAZE MADNESS

How fast can you get through this maddening maze?

Answer on page 85.

HERE KITTY, KITTY

There's a CAT in each word below. Fill in the blanks with the right letters to make words that answer the clues.

1. C O A T — jacket
2. C H A T I E R — talk rapidly
3. C A R T — wagon
4. C O A S T E R — carnival ride, roller ___
5. C A R R O T S — orange veggies
6. C A R P E T — rug
7. C A T E H E R — baseball player
8. S C A T — Get out of here!
9. S C A R L E T — shade of red
10. C A B I N E T — place to store things
11. C A F I T E R I A — eating area in a school
12. C H A R I O T — horse-drawn vehicle of ancient times
13. C H E A T E R — dishonest person
14. C A P I T A L — uppercase letter
15. C A R T O O N — short animated film

Answers on page 87.

SEE THE U.S.A.

The name of a state is hidden between two or three words in these silly sentences. Underline each state name as you locate it.

1. THE KIDS CAN COLOR A DOZEN PICTURES.

2. WHAT'S THE MAIN EVENT?

3. THE TRIO WANTED TO PERFORM.

4. DID AL ASK ABOUT ME?

5. ARE THERE ANY MORE GONDOLAS?

6. THEY MIGHT MISS OUR INTERVIEW.

7. HE WENT OUT WITHOUT A HAT.

8. THAT WAS OVER MONTHS AGO.

9. THE DOCTOR AT A LAB AMAZED US.

10. THEY ALL WATCHED WHEN EVA DANCED.

Answers on page 87.

THE WRONG TRACK

Fill in the missing two letters in each word below. The letters you fill in—if you read down the column—will form the answer to this riddle: Why did the boy take his dog to the railroad station?

1. Way to serve potatoes   M A S **H E** D

2. Breakfast food   W A F F L E S

3. Go inside   E N T E R

4. Formal suit for a man   T U X E D O

5. Fictional tale   S _ _ R Y

6. Avenue   S T R E E T

7. Steps   S T A I R S

8. Sad   U N H A P P Y

9. A sour green fruit   L I M E

Answers on page 85.

SLIGHT CHANGE

In the example below, the underlined letters in each word have been changed to form a riddle and answer that make sense. Now, you change the underlined letters, one per word, in the rest of these silly questions and answers to discover the riddles and get the jokes!

Example: <u>T</u>HAT <u>G</u>OES <u>I</u> DANGE<u>R</u> <u>B</u>RINK?
What does a dancer drink?

T<u>I</u>P WA<u>F</u>ER
Tap water.

1. WH<u>O</u> D<u>A</u>D <u>S</u>HE B<u>A</u>Y <u>F</u>IT <u>I</u>N HI<u>M</u> <u>M</u>ATCH?

Who did   ne B y il n hi   atch

H<u>I</u> <u>P</u>ANTED <u>G</u>O <u>M</u>E O<u>F</u> <u>D</u>IME.

_____

2. WH<u>I</u>T DI<u>N</u> O<u>R</u>E WAL<u>K</u> <u>D</u>AY <u>G</u>O <u>S</u>HE OT<u>TE</u>R WAL<u>K</u>?

_____

<u>A</u> <u>S</u>ILL <u>B</u>EET YO<u>N</u> <u>I</u>T TH<u>Y</u> CORNE<u>D</u>.

_____

3. WH<u>ET</u> <u>M</u>IND <u>I</u>F <u>B</u>ET <u>M</u>AN <u>S</u>OU KEE<u>N</u> <u>ON</u> <u>I</u> JAR?

_____

<u>I</u> <u>F</u>AR <u>B</u>ET.

_____

Answers on page 87.

SEW WHAT?

Use only the letters S-E-W (in any order) to find the words.

Opposite of sour	S W E ET
Direction on a map	W E S T
Perspire	S W E AT
Seven-day periods	W E E K S
Does the laundry	W A S H E S
Unwanted plants	W E E D S
Smarter	W S E R
Reply	A N S W E R
Scandinavian country	S W E D E N
Christmas decorations	W R E A T H S

Answers on page 86.

PICTURE CROSSWORD

Name each picture, and write it in the numbered space going **ACROSS** or **DOWN**.

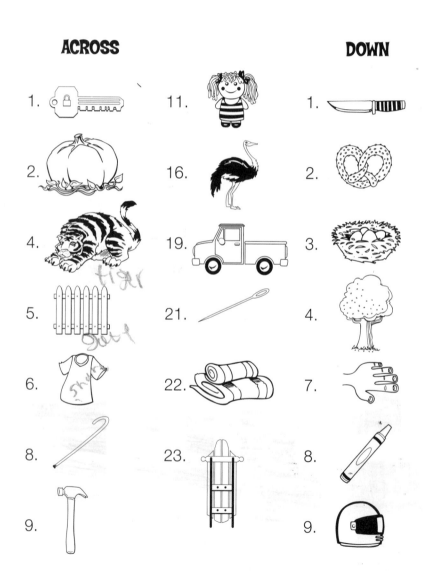

ACROSS

1.

2.

4.

5.

6.

8.

9.

11.

16.

19.

21.

22.

23.

DOWN

1.

2.

3.

4.

7.

8.

9.

10.

14.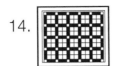

18.

12.

15.

20.

13.

17.

18

COLOR COORDINATED

Find nineteen exotic colors in this grid. Look up, down, and diagonally and both forward and backward. Circle each color when you find it.

AQUA	ECRU	PEARL	TAN
CREAM	EMERALD	PLATINUM	TEAL
CRIMSON	JADE	PUCE	TOPAZ
CYAN	LILAC	PUMPKIN	UMBER
DUN	MAGENTA	ROSE	

Answers on page 85.

TEAM MATES

Circle the two pictures that are exactly the same.

A

B

C

D

E

F

G

H

I

Answers on page 86.

SO SYMBOL

Spell out each character, then place it in the correct blank space below to form a word or phrase that completes each sentence.

$$- \quad \sqrt{} \quad \triangle \quad \square \quad @ \quad * \quad \& \quad + \quad , \quad :$$

1. The goal in chess is to ___√___ mate your opponent's king.
2. Dining rooms are often lit by crystal ch___&___eliers hung from the ceiling.
3. The car's instruments and controls are on the _____ board.
4. The St___@___ue of Liberty symbolizes freedom and democracy.
5. "The ___*___-Spangled Banner" is the national anthem of the U.S.A.
6. In an orchestra, the ___△___ is a small instrument that makes a "ding" sound.
7. ___□___ dances are lively social events.
8. Toddlers often carry around their stuffed animals or _____ h toys.
9. A lieutenant _____ el is an army officer.
10. One of the president's titles is _____ nder in Chief.

STINGER

Write one letter in the blank space on each line to form a nine-letter word. Then read down the column to find the three-word answer to this riddle: What does a bee wear?

G Y M N A S I U M

E V E R Y B O D Y

W E D N E S D A Y

G E N T L E M A N

B R I L L I A N T

M I C R O W A V E

S T O P W A T C H

O V E R J O Y E D

E N C H A N T E D

A D J E C T I V E

S T O C K R O O M

E X T R E M E L Y

Q U A R T E R L Y

Answers on page 89.

TEE TIME

There was not enough space to write out the whole name and city on these T-shirts—there was room for only three letters on each line. The letters on the top line are part of the city's name, and the letters on the bottom line are part of the state's name. Can you name all these American cities? Use the hints on page 23 to guide you.

Example: _ _LAN_ _ is ATLANTA
            _ _ ORG_ _ is GEORGIA

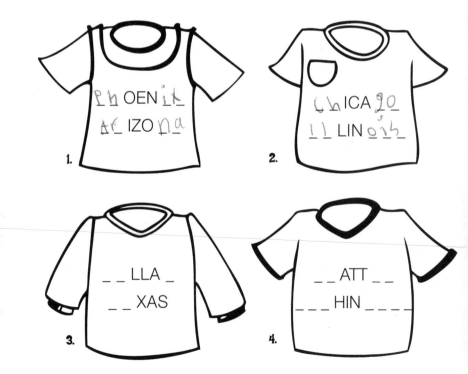

1. Ph OEN ix
   Ar IZO na

2. Ch ICA go
   Il LIN ois

3. _ _ LLA _
   _ _ XAS

4. _ _ ATT _ _
   _ _ _ HIN _ _ _ _

HINTS

Big "D"

Coffee capital of the world

Founded during a gold strike

Home of many theme parks

Major city in the Aloha state

Named for the sixteenth president

Capital of the Grand Canyon state

Its main attraction is the
    Inner Harbor

The Mile-High City

The Windy City

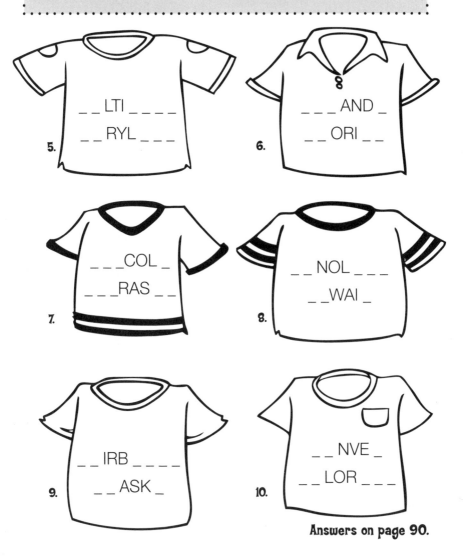

5. _ _ LTI _ _ _ _ / _ _ RYL _ _ _

6. _ _ _ AND _ / _ _ ORI _ _

7. _ _ _ COL _ / _ _ _ RAS _ _

8. _ _ NOL _ _ _ / _ _ WAI _

9. _ _ IRB _ _ _ _ / _ _ ASK _

10. _ _ NVE _ / _ _ LOR _ _ _

Answers on page 90.

FORTUNE COOKIES

Oops! The riddles and answers for a new batch of fortune cookies were accidentally split in half. Can you look among the pieces to find the two pieces for each riddle and the two pieces that form their answers? Write them on the blank lines below.

_____

_____

_____

_____

BANKS.

BECAUSE THE FARMER

DOES A SKUNK HAVE?

FOLD IT

HOW MUCH MONEY

IN HALF.

HAVE MONEY?

KEEP THEIR MONEY?

IN MEMORY

MILKS THEM DRY.

ONE

WHAT'S THE FASTEST WAY

WHERE DO COMPUTERS

TO DOUBLE YOUR MONEY?

WHY DON'T COWS

SCENT.

Answers on page 88.

ADD A LETTER

Add one letter to each line, then rearrange the letters to make words that answer the clues.

O   The 15th letter of the alphabet

o f   Word that's used with "either"

o r e   Material found in mines

R o s e   Flower with thorns

s o r e s   Open cuts

s n o r e s   Loud sleep noises

s e r m o n s   Speeches in churches

m o n s t e r s   Scary creatures

SCRAMBLED GO-TOGETHERS

Unscramble the two words between "and" to find a pair of things that go together.

Example: OCLK and EKY = LOCK and KEY

1. COBM and SHRUB = _Com B_ and _Brush_

2. REHAMM and NILA = _hammer_ and _nail_

3. LEENED and THEADR = _neelned_ and _thread_

4. ALIP and HOLEVS = _Pali_ and _shovle_

5. UCP and CERASU = _Cup_ and _Saucer_

6. APREP and LICENP = _Papper_ and _pencil_

7. FINEK and RFOK = _knife_ and _frok_

8. WOB and RWAOR = _Bow_ and _arwaroi_

Answers on page 88.

PICTURE RIDDLE

Fill in the blanks with words that define the pictures. Then take the letters that are above the numbered spaces and copy them to the matching numbered spaces in the answer section at the bottom of the page. The sentence you get will answer this riddle: What do baseball and pancakes have in common?

A.
e y e s
3 12 22

E.
c h e r r y
    2   23 9 4

B.
B e l l
18 10   11

F.
h o u s e
8 6

C.
S t a m p
   20 19

G.
S h e e p
   16

D.
B o t t l e
5 13 15 21   17

H.
t e n t
1   14 7

Answer:

t h e y   B o t h   c a l y
1 2 3 4   5 6 7 8   9 10 11 12

o n   t h e   B a t t e l.
13 14   15 16 17   18 19 20 21 22 23

Answers on page 89.

DO-IT-YOURSELF

Fill the grid with words that begin with "D." Start with the given letters and work from there until there are no empty spaces left.

3 Letters
DAD
DAY
DOE

4 Letters
DEAL
DEER
DOLL
DRAG
DYED

5 Letters
DANDY
DAWNS
DINER
DODGE
DOUGH
DOZED

6 Letters
DIPPER
DISHES
DRAFTY

7 Letters
DOODLED
DRESSES

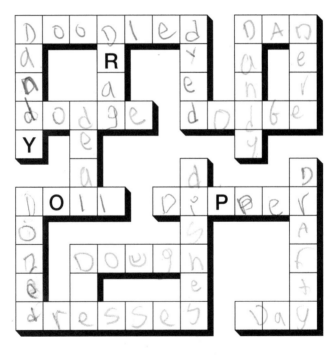

Answers on page 89.

OUT OF SIGHT

Pictures of eight things you could pack in your carry-on luggage are hidden in the airport scene on the opposite page. Can you find all of them?

Answers on page 90.

FOOTBALL FUN

Find and circle the sixteen football terms in the list. Look up, down, and diagonally, both forward and backward. Then read the leftover letters in the grid, from left to right and top to bottom. Without changing the order, write the letters in the blank spaces on the opposite page to get the answer to this riddle: What do you get when you cross a telephone with a very big football player?

COACH

DEFENSE

GOAL LINE

GUARD

HUDDLE

IN BOUNDS

KICK

LINE JUDGE

LINEMAN

OFFENSE

REFEREE

ROOKIE

SUPER BOWL

TACKLE

TEAM

ZONE

C	S	U	P	E	R	B	O	W	L
A	O	W	M	I	D	F	E	I	I
D	R	A	U	G	F	R	N	N	N
E	E	R	C	E	E	E	I	B	E
T	C	S	N	H	M	F	L	O	J
A	E	S	N	A	I	E	L	U	U
C	E	V	N	E	E	R	A	N	D
K	I	C	K	R	F	E	O	D	G
L	R	O	O	K	I	E	G	S	E
E	Z	O	N	E	L	D	D	U	H

Answer:

_ _ _ _ _ _ _ _ _ _ _ _

Answers on page 94.

JUSTICE IS SERVED

Write the answer to each clue in the numbered blank spaces. Then copy the letters to the answer box on the opposite page. The letters you place in the answer box should be the same ones that are above the numbered blanks in the puzzle section. In other words, the letter you write above the 11 in the clue should be the same letter you write over the 11 in the answer section. Work back and forth between the clues and the answer box to find a riddle and its answer.

CLUES

1. The sixth month

J̲ U̲ N̲ e̲
11 20 21 3

2. Not costing anything

f̲ r̲ e̲ e̲
27 34 5 16

3. Walk in water

W̲ a̲ d̲ e̲
1 17 6 15

4. Not on time

l̲ a̲ t̲ e̲
19 26 25 8

5. Fizzy drink

S̲ O̲ d̲ a̲
9 28 30 10

6. Crabby person (like Oscar)

g̲ r̲ o̲ u̲ c̲ h̲
14 4 7 33 22 23

7. Feel

t̲ o̲ u̲ c̲ h̲
18 32 12 31 2

8. Frog's relative

t̲ o̲ a̲ d̲
35 29 24 13

where does a
1 2 3 4 5   6 7 8 9   10

judge
11 12 13 14 15

eat lunch?
16 17 18   19 20 21 22 23

at a food court.
24 25 26   27 28 29 30   31 32 33 34 35

Answers on page 92.

FACES IN THE CROWD

A set of triplets is hiding in this picture. How quickly can you find the three identical faces in this crowd?

Answer on page 93.

STEP BY STEP

Start at the circled letter in the grid and move one square at a time to find a riddle and its answer. Move straight across, up, or down, but *not* diagonally. When you find a letter, write it in the blank spaces below and cross it off in the grid. All letters and symbols in the grid will be used only once.

T	C	O	O
S	R	B	-
O	Y	A	B
H	?	D	O
G	I	A	O
E	T	H	.
H	I	D	Y
T	D	(W)	H

W**hy** d**i**d
the gh**o**st
c r y?
It had a
B O O - B o o .

Answer on page 86.

DOUBLE TROUBLE

Separate the word list into two categories, birds and fish. Then put the words into the grids. Each grid should contain only words from one category. Letters are already placed in each grid to get you started.

ALBACORE
ANCHOVY
CANARY
DOVE
EAGLE
EEL
FLOUNDER
HAWK
ORIOLE
OSTRICH
PERCH
PIGEON
RAY
SOLE
TROUT
TUNA

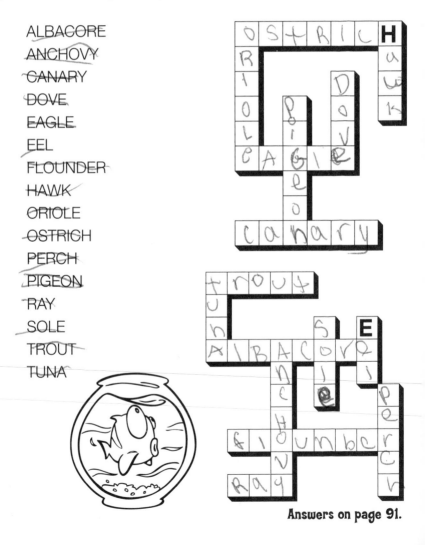

Answers on page 91.

FOUR FITS

Place the words from the box into the blanks on the lines below to make words that fit the clues. Each of the words is used only once.

ARCH	AUNT	HAIR	LASS	MAIN
OVER	PEAR	ROAD	SPIT	THEN

1. H O _SPIT_ A L — doctor's workplace

2. C _HAIR_ M A N — person who conducts a meeting

3. S E _ARCH_ E D — looked for

4. G _OVER_ N O R — head of a state

5. H _AUNT_ E D — like some Halloween houses

6. R E _MAIN_ D E R — whatever's left over

7. C L _ASS_ R O O M — area in a school

8. B _ROAD_ W A Y — famous Manhattan street

9. S _PEAR_ M I N T — chewing gum flavor

10. A U _THEN_ T I C — genuine

Answers on page 90.

IF THE SHOE FITS

Circle eight differences between the picture on this page and the picture on the opposite page.

$18.89

Answers on page 96.

BODY BUILDING PLUS

Do the math by adding some letters to each body part and then scrambling the letters to form a word that fits the clue.

Example: WRIST + REL = baton experts   **TWIRLERS**

1. BROW + INE = chocolate dessert   *Browine*

2. HAND + OSUTS = numbers
higher than 999

3. TOE + SYR = shellfish that
makes pearls   _____

4. KNEE + RASS = sporty shoes   _____

5. HEART + LE = jacket material   _____

6. NOSE + TRA = congress person   _____

7. CHIN + SEE = Asian language   _____

8. LIPS + REM = easier   _____

Now, subtract some letters from each body part and scramble them to form a word that fits the clue.

Example: STOMACH – HAC = maximum   **MOST**

9. FINGER – NG = blaze   _____

10. SHOULDER – DOLE = hurry   _____

11. EYELASH – YES = cure   _____

12. MOUTH – UM = scorching   _____

13. NOSTRIL – STR = wild animal _____

14. ANKLE – K = path   _____

15. MUSCLE – SM = hint   _____

16. RIBCAGE – GAE = infant's bed _____

Answers on page 91.

SQUISH/SQUASH

Two items from the same category are squished together on each line. All the letters in each word are in the correct order—you just have to separate them.

Example: P C A E R R A S O T S = PEAS & CARROTS

   Here are the categories of squished words, but they're not listed in the correct order!

CATEGORIES

Cheeses

Coins

Languages

Months of the year

Numbers

Occupations

Olympic sports

Relatives

Rooms in a house

Zoo animals

1. C G R A O U N D F S I N A T H E R

   _____ & _____

2. M N O A R V E M C B E R H

   _____ & _____

3. S W C O T I S T A S G E

   _____ & _____

4. P I L N U O R S E T

   _____ & _____

5. S E T H I V E R T N Y

   _____ & _____

6. E L E W O P H A L F N T

   _____ & _____

7. K I B E T C D R H E N O O M

   _____ & _____

8. D I P E M N N Y E

   _____ & _____

9. A R C B O H E R X I N G Y

   _____ & _____

10. D E N G U T L I C H S H

    _____ & _____

Answers on page 95.

RIDDLE CROSSWORD

Write the answers to each clue in the spaces in the grid, either **ACROSS** or **DOWN**. Then fill in the numbered blanks below the grid with the letters in the numbered squares. When you have finished, you will have the answer to this riddle: How do you unlock a haunted house?

ACROSS

1. Is fond of
4. Stuff inside pens
6. Opposite of dry
7. A female relative
8. An item in Santa's bag
9. Opposite of no
11. Opposite of exit
13. Long, long ___ (in the past)
15. The food that horses eat
16. Frame for holding artwork

DOWN

1. Opposite of high
2. Nickname for a baby cat
3. Grainy material at the beach
4. Type of cube used in cold drinks
5. Holds on to
8. Molars and incisors
9. Periods of 365 days
10. One of the Great Lakes
12. Make an effort to do something
14. Bird that hoots

Crossword Puzzle

Answer:

$\overline{}_{6}$ $\overline{}_{4}$ $\overline{}_{12}$ $\overline{}_{15}$ $\overline{}_{13}$ $\overline{}_{3}$ $\overline{}_{5}$ $\overline{}_{16}$ $\overline{}_{1}$ $\overline{}_{10}$ $\overline{}_{8}$ $\overline{}_{14}$ $\overline{}_{7}$ $\overline{}_{2}$ $\overline{}_{11}$ $\overline{}_{9}$

Answers on page 92.

WATCH IT!

Find and circle the twenty-one dog items in the list below. Look up, down, and diagonally, both forward and backward. Then read the letters in the grid that have not been circled, reading from left to right and top to bottom. Without changing the order, write them in the blank spaces below to find the answer to this riddle: What happens to a dog that swallows a watch?

BED	CLIPPER	HOUSE
BLANKET	COAT	I.D. TAG
BONE	COLLAR	LEASH
BOWL	COMB	RAMP
BRUSH	CRATE	SHAMPOO
CAP	GATE	SWEATER
CARRIER	HARNESS	TOY

```
C O L L A R I H T G
A G O T E K N A L B
R A M P H S U R B E
R T T S M A L N E S
I E I D T A G E D W
E T A O C O H S H E
R B C B T R C S O A
O Y O T F T A I U T
C N M W K E P T S E
E S B C L I P P E R
```

_ _ _ _ _ _ _ _ _ _ _ _ _ _ _

Answers on page 93.

INSTANT MESSAGING

Do your own instant messaging by adding IM to each word in the box to make a new word that fits one of the clues. IM can be added anywhere in the word—beginning, middle, or end. The first one was done for you.

AGE	**ESTATE**	**ME**	**PRESS**
DECAL	**GRACE**	**PORT**	~~**SON**~~
DEN	**LIT**	**POSE**	**TED**

1. "Simple" guy <u>SIMON</u>

2. Used a stopwatch _____

3. Picture _____

4. Jeans material _____

5. Rough guess _____

6. Type of point (math) _____

7. Frown _____

8. Bring goods into a country _____

9. Gain someone's admiration _____

10. Take unfair advantage _____

11. Boundary line _____

12. Actor who doesn't use words _____

Answers on page 92.

DOUBLE-ACTING WORDS

One word will answer each set of clues. Write the double-acting word in the blank space.

Example: New York baseball player + famous children's song "___ Doodle" = **Answer:** YANKEE

1. Soil + our planet = _____

2. Pale + what a lamp gives off = _____

3. Take part in a game + stage show = _____

4. Loud noise + tennis player's equipment = _____

5. An increase in salary + lift up = _____

6. Young goat + tease = _____

7. Billiards game + swimming place = _____

8. Very uncommon + cooked just a little bit = _____

9. A thin cushion + a writing tablet = _____

10. Color on the U.S. flag + sad = _____

Answers on page 89.

ANNA GRAM

Anna Gram likes to take all the letters of one word and scramble them to form a new word. Help her out by rearranging all the letters in each word and writing them into the grid **ACROSS** and **DOWN**. Make sure that the word you put into the grid has the same number as the listed word. One word has been rearranged for you.

ACROSS

1. HEART
3. PANEL
5. HEAT
7. CHIN
8. NIP
10. VASE
12. DAWN
13. ARC

DOWN

1. ACHE
2. CANOE
3. CHEAP
4. PLEASE
6. SKIS
9. EARN
11. DEN

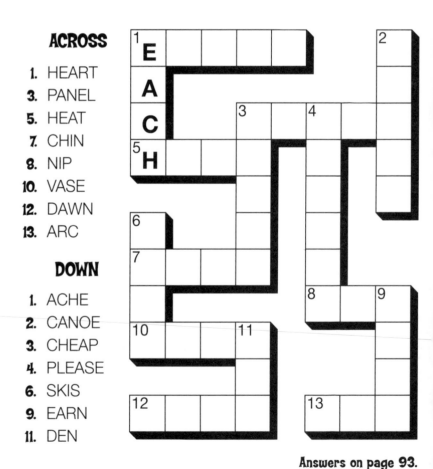

BEAUTY TREATMENT

Put the nine words that are scattered across the page into the grid in alphabetical order. Then read the circled letters from left to right and top to bottom to get the answer to this riddle: How do rabbits fix their hair?

PEACHES

PRUDENT

PUBLISH

PAUSING

PREPARE

PANTHER

PUZZLES

PASSKEY

PROVERB

1.
2.
3.
4.
5.
6.
7.
8.
9.

Answer:

_____

Answers on page 95.

AUTHOR! AUTHOR!

Match each "author" with his or her book by drawing a line between the name and the book title.

AUTHOR   **BOOK TITLE**

Sir Gerry

R. T. Choke

Mr. E. Mann

Vy Olin

A. King

May Cup

Al E. Katz

Answers on page 91.

A TRICKY SITUATION

The word in the right column uses all the letters of the word in the left column *except* for one. Write the missing letter in the middle column. Then write the letters in the blank spaces below so that they match the numbers in parentheses. You will find a three-word expression that describes a situation when you're not sure what the outcome will be.

CUSHIONS	___	(5)	COUSINS
TROUBLES	___	(10)	BUTLERS
INVESTOR	___	(1)	VERSION
GREETING	___	(9)	INTEGER
EVIDENCE	___	(7)	DECEIVE
ORIGINAL	___	(2)	RAILING
DYNAMITE	___	(8)	ANYTIME
CIRCUSES	___	(4)	CRUISES
AWARDING	___	(6)	DRAWING
NUISANCE	___	(3)	CANINES

 __ __ __ __ __   __ __ __   __ __
 1 2 3 4 5   6 7 8   9 10

Answers on page 93.

NOT THE SAME OLD GRIND

Decipher this code to find a riddle and its answer.

A = ▲	N = ❯
B = Ω	O = ◆
C = ★	P = ←
D = ◣	Q = ✂
E = ±	R = ✉
F = ⇨	S = ▽
G = ❀	T = ■
H = ◆	U = ☆
I = ←	V = Ø
J = ◁	W = √
K = ☛	X = △
L = ◯	Y = ◀
M = ☎	Z = "

√ ◆ ▲ ■   ◄ ← ◄   ■ ◆ ±

WHAT DID The

◄ ± ❯ ■ ← ▽ ■   ▽ ± ±   ▲ ■

Dentist see At

■ ◆ ±   ❯ ◆ ⊠ ■ ◆   ◄ ◆ ⊘ ±?

the north PoLe?

▲   ☎ ◆ ⊘ ▲ ⊠   Ω ± ▲ ⊠.

A MoLAr BehC.

Answer on page 92.

HELP WANTED

Match the want ad on this page with the job seeker on the opposite page. Write the correct letter of the answer in the space next to each ad.

1. You can nail this job if you're handy with a file.   _____

2. Want a new leash on life? Apply now.   _____

3. Star search. Must be a night person.   _____

4. Wanted: sum person to solve problems.   _____

5. Seeking someone who serves well.   _____

6. Call if you wood prefer to work outdoors.   _____

7. Pressing need for a person without wrinkles.   _____

8. Seas the opportunity to travel.   _____

A

B

C

D

E

F

G

H

Answers on page 88.

CLASSROOM CAPER

Circle the eight things that are wrong here.

MEMORY QUIZ

Study the picture on this page for 60 seconds, and then turn to the next page to answer some questions about it.

How many questions can you answer about the park scene on the previous page? No looking back!

1. How many children are playing volleyball?

_____

2. Who is rowing the boat—the woman or the girl?

_____

3. What kind of flowers are pictured?

_____

4. What board game is being played?

_____

5. How many fish are in the bucket?

_____

6. Which boy is reeling in a fish—the shorter one or the taller one?

_____

7. What is the girl in the rowboat wearing on her head?

_____

8. Is it a cloudy or a sunny day?

_____

9. Are there any squirrels in the scene? If so, how many?

_____

10. What kind of dogs are being walked?

_____

Answers on page 94.

WELL-VERSED

A well-versed person knows a lot about a subject. Here's your chance to show off your knowledge. Each clue below contains two words, and the clue words rhyme with their matching answer words. In addition, the words in each answer are related to each other. All you have to do is change one letter in each of the clue words.

Example: YEAR and BAR = NEAR and FAR

1. NOT and BOLD = _____

2. HOOD and LAD = _____

3. SHIN and MAT = _____

4. SORE and MESS = _____

5. DOVE and DATE = _____

6. PAST and GLOW = _____

7. FIGHT and SAY = _____

8. BARGE and STALL = _____

Answers on page 94.

FLOWER BED

Place each flower on a horizontal line in the grid below. If the name is more than one word, do not leave blank spaces between the words. If the name is hyphenated, do not insert the hyphens. Each name fits exactly on one line only. When the grid is full, read down one of the columns to find the name of another flower.

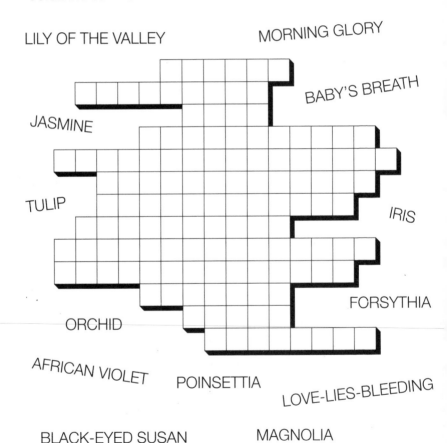

LILY OF THE VALLEY

MORNING GLORY

BABY'S BREATH

JASMINE

TULIP

IRIS

FORSYTHIA

ORCHID

AFRICAN VIOLET   POINSETTIA

LOVE-LIES-BLEEDING

BLACK-EYED SUSAN   MAGNOLIA

Answers on page 96.

DIZZY DEFINITIONS

Match the words in the left column with the dizzy definitions in the right column. Don't think of the real meaning of the words. Instead, break down each word into two parts.

Example: BROADCAST = wide acting group (broad + cast)

1. FOOTNOTE		**A.**	it's my turn to pass out the cards
2. HERRING		**B.**	look at the tool
3. KIDNAPPING		**C.**	skinny bird home
4. MANGO		**D.**	the girl's jewelry
5. SEESAW		**E.**	sickness hut
6. THINNEST		**F.**	message on the bottom of a leg
7. FLUSHED		**G.**	king's neckwear
8. CARNATION		**H.**	baby's asleep
9. ROYALTIES		**I.**	auto country
10. IDEAL		**J.**	guy, scram!

Answers on page 91.

DRIVING HAZARD

Why are geese such bad drivers? To find out why, put each car part into the grid. Two letters have been placed to start you off. When the puzzle is complete, read the circled letters from left to right and top to bottom and you'll have the answer.

4 Letters
AXLE
BODY
TIRE

7 Letters
MUFFLER
SUNROOF

5 Letters
BRAKE
PEDAL
RADIO
TRUNK

8 Letters
CYLINDER
MUD GUARD

6 Letters
BUMPER
CLUTCH
ENGINE
HEATER
OIL PAN
TOW BAR

10 Letters
THERMOSTAT

Answer:

Answers on page 89.

CLEANING UP

Read each clue and cross off its matching word on the opposite page. Then write the leftover words, from left to right and top to bottom, on the line. They won't make any sense. But . . . change just one letter in each word to answer this riddle: Why doesn't Saturn like to take a bath?

CLUES

1. Cute
2. Soccer player
3. Small guitar
4. Worth tons of money
5. Japanese art of self-defense
6. Hot cereal
7. Type of bean or fish
8. Cry like a baby
9. Marionette
10. Halloween month
11. Running event
12. Bank worker
13. Nothing
14. Use a keyboard
15. Large cat

UKULELE	AT	PUPPET	VALUABLE
RACE	OATMEAL	RIGHT	TYPE
OCTOBER	GOALIE	BAWL	HEAVE
I	ZILCH	LEOPARD	JELLY
KARATE	TELLER	WING	ADORABLE

Leftover words: _____

Change one letter in each word: _____

Answers on page 94.

MISSING LINKS

Take a word from the list on this page and add it to one of the letter groups on the opposite page. If you insert it in the right place, it will form the end of the first word *and* the start of the second word.

Example: Place THE on the first line to make TEE<u>THE</u> and <u>THE</u>IRS.

AGE	FIN	SET
ANT	LET	TEN
CAT	OUT	~~THE~~
DEN	PEN	TON

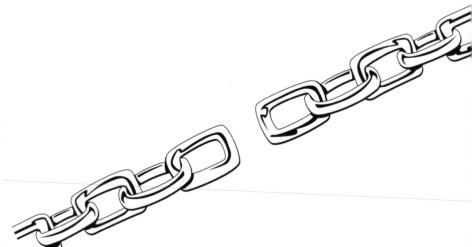

1. TEE <u>THE</u> IRS

2. COT _____ GUE

3. DAM _____ NCY

4. CLO _____ TLE

5. MUF _____ ISH

6. SUD _____ TAL

7. HAP _____ CIL

8. SPR _____ FIT

9. FAS _____ DER

10. INF _____ LER

11. VIO _____ TER

12. BOB _____ NAP

Answers on page 95.

IT'S NOT WHAT YOU SAY . . .

It's how you say it. Each of the following ten boxes contains words and/or letters that create coded messages. Look at the size of the letters and words, the direction they're facing, and other visual clues to unlock their secrets.

Example: ban   ana = banana split

1.
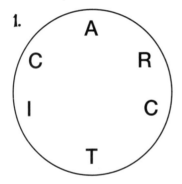

2.

E H C A

_____

3.

D I V I S I O N

_____

4.

MISS MUFFET

_____

5.

GEGS

6.

LAMOTHERW

7.

TECH

8.

OVERS

---

9. FIVE

10.

STEP IT

Answers on page 90.

SHAPE UP

Three riddles and answers are mixed up here. First, separate the words according to the shapes they are inside. Second, rearrange them so that they make sense and write them down in the space provided on the opposite page. Third, laugh your head off.

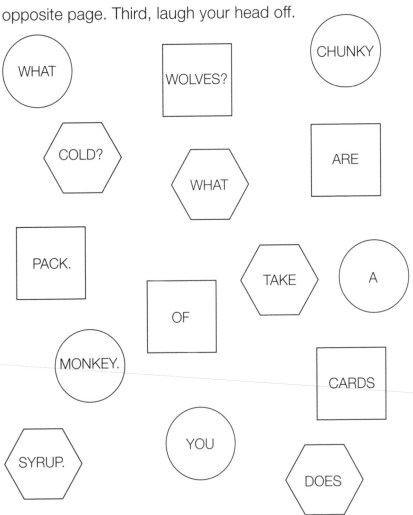

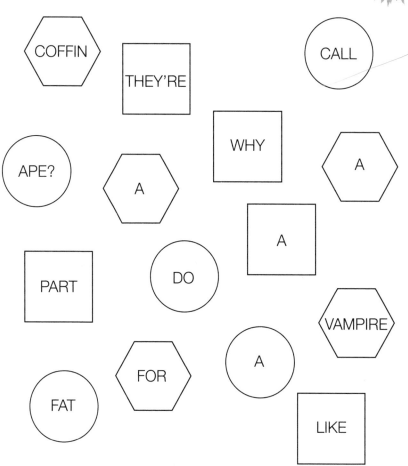

COFFIN

THEY'RE

CALL

WHY

APE?

A

A

A

PART

DO

VAMPIRE

FOR

A

FAT

LIKE

Answers on page 88.

EXCUSES, EXCUSES

The students in Mr. Cal Q. Lator's math class thought up a bunch of creative excuses for not handing in their homework assignments. But one mischievous kid tore the excuses apart and made a list of twenty-four words. Put each word back in the correct spot so that the "excuses" make sense.

AND	BUS	CASE	CUE	DENT	DROWN
END	FAT	HAM	HEN	HI	HOME
HUG	JUMP	MOTH	OFF	PARENTS	PILL
PORT	RIP	TO	WE	WED	WIN

1. MY _ _ _ STER CHE_ _ _ _ IT.

2. I _ _ _ _ _ED IN_ _ A LAKE TO RES_ _ _ _ MY FRI_ _ _ _ AND MY _ _ _ _WORK _ _ _ _ _ _ED.

3. A _ _ _ _E GUST OF _ _ _ _D BLEW IT OUT OF MY H_ _ _ _S W_ _ _LE WE _ _RE DRIVING MY GRAND_ _ _ _ _ _ _ _ _ TO THE AIR_ _ _ _ _.

4. MY _ _ _ _HER ACCI_ _ _ _ _ALLY PUT IT IN HIS BRIEF_ _ _ _ _ W_ _ _ _ HE WENT ON A _ _ _ _INESS T_ _ _ _.

5. MY_ _ _ _ _ER S_ _ _ _ _ED C_ _ _ _EE ALL OVER IT.

Answers on page 95.

BEFORE OR AFTER

In the coded sentences that follow, change each letter to the one immediately **BEFORE** or **AFTER** it in the alphabet to find a riddle and answer. Use this guide.

A B C D E F G H I J K L M N O P Q R S T U V W X Y Z

VGZ   BSD   UBLQJSFT   VOQPQTKBS?

_____

CFDBTRD   UGFX   BSD   B   QBHM

_____

JM   SID   MDBJ.

_____

Now, do it again to find another riddle and answer.

VIBS KHWFR JO UGD XBUFQ

_____

BMC SBJDT XNT BMZXGFQD

_____

ZPV VBOS SP FN?

_____

B UBWJ BSBA.

_____

Answers on page 94.

PUNNY WORDS

Fill in the blank space in each of the sentences by using the words on this page. It helps to think "punny." To get you started, we've done the first one for you.

DELIGHT	OLIVE
DESPAIR	PECAN
DISCARD	POLICE
~~GORILLA~~	SPIDER
ICON	TURNIP
LEAF	WATER

1. Would you <u>GORILLA</u> hot dog for me on the barbecue?

2. Anything you can do _____ do better.

3. Go away! Just _____ me alone.

4. I will buy _____ for my friend's birthday.

5. _____ you going to be when you grow up?

6. _____ tire is in the trunk of the car.

7. You should _____ the heat in the winter.

8. It's getting dark, so please switch on _____.

9. _____ in a brand-new house.

10. Don't tease the small kid. _____ someone your own size.

11. It's polite to say _____ and thank you.

12. He _____ hiding behind the tree.

Answers on page 94.

ENCYCLOPEDIA WORDS*

Put each word in the grid. Use the starting letters and work from there until the grid is complete.

3 Letters
AND
CAN
NAP
ONE

4 Letters
AIDE
CLIP
DIAL
ONLY
PAIN
PILE
YELP

5 Letters
ALIEN
ALONE
DAILY
DECOY
DELAY
PIANO
PIECE
YIELD

6 Letters
CANDLE
EYELID
POLICE

7 Letters
CLEANED
CYCLONE
DECLINE
PANELED
PELICAN

*Each word in the list is spelled with only the letters found in the word *encyclopedia*.

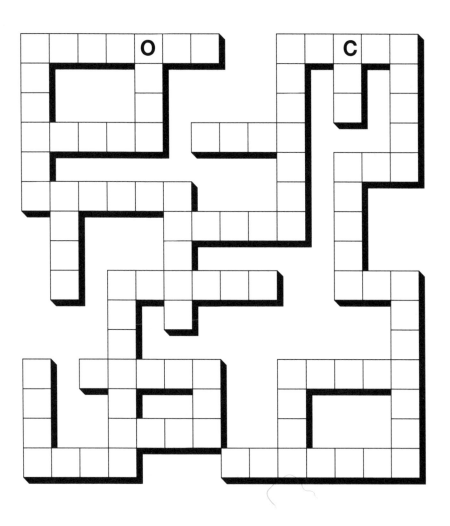

Answers on page 96.

CHANGE OVER

Each word in the list is an anagram—a word that can be rearranged to spell an entirely different word, like BAKER and BREAK. Rearrange the letters in each word in the list below to find a new word, and then write the new word in the grid. When all the spaces in the grid are filled in, read down the starred column to find something that is always changing.

1. THAW
2. FLESH
3. BEING
4. WARD
5. BAKER
6. PALM
7. NIGHT
8. SHRUB
9. THERE
10. REEF

Answers on page 91.

ANSWERS

EASY AS PIE (pg. 5)

THE WRONG TRACK (pg. 13)

1. MAS<u>HED</u>
2.   <u>WA</u>FFLES
3.   <u>EN</u>TER
4. TUX<u>ED</u>O
5.   S<u>T</u>ORY
6.   ST<u>R</u>EET
7.   ST<u>AI</u>RS
8.   UN<u>H</u>APPY
9.   L<u>IME</u>

Answer: He wanted to train him.

COLOR COORDINATED (pg.18)

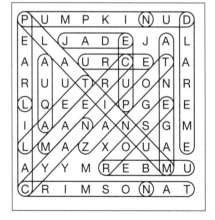

MAZE MADNESS (pg. 10)

MAGIC SQUARES (pg. 6)

A

O	P	E	N
P	A	N	E
E	N	D	S
N	E	S	T

B

G	R	A	B
R	O	P	E
A	P	E	S
B	E	S	T

C

T	O	P	S
O	V	A	L
P	A	P	A
S	L	A	P

D

S	N	O	W
N	I	N	E
O	N	C	E
W	E	E	D

STEP BY STEP (pg. 37)
Why did the ghost cry?
It had a boo-boo.

SEW WHAT? (pg. 15)
SWEET
WEST
SWEAT
WEEKS
WASHES
WISER
WEEDS
ANSWER
SWEDEN
WREATHS

TEAMMATES (pg. 19)

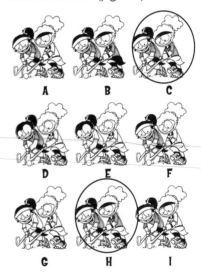

A B C

D E F

G H I

HERE KITTY, KITTY (pg. 11)

1. COAT
2. CHATTER
3. CART
4. COASTER
5. CARROTS
6. CARPET
7. CATCHER
8. SCAT
9. SCARLET
10. CABINET
11. CAFETERIA
12. CHARIOT
13. CHEATER
14. CAPITAL
15. CARTOON

PICTURE CROSSWORD (pg. 16)

SLIGHT CHANGE (pg. 14)

1. Why did the boy sit on his watch? He wanted to be on time.
2. What did one wall say to the other wall? I will meet you at the corner.
3. What kind of pet can you keep in a car? A car pet.

SEE THE U.S.A. (pg. 12)

1. THE KIDS CAN <u>COLOR A DOZ</u>EN PICTURES.
2. WHAT'S THE <u>MAIN E</u>VENT?
3. THE TR<u>IO WAN</u>TED TO PERFORM.
4. DID <u>AL ASK A</u>BOUT ME?
5. ARE THERE ANY M<u>ORE GON</u>DOLAS?
6. THEY MIGHT <u>MISS OUR I</u>NTERVIEW.
7. HE WENT OUT WITH<u>OUT A HAT</u>.
8. THAT WAS <u>OVER MONTH</u>S AGO.
9. THE DOCTOR AT <u>A LAB AMAZED</u> US.
10. THEY ALL WATCHED WHE<u>N EVA DA</u>NCED.

SO SYMBOL (pg. 20)

1. <u>Check</u>mate
2. Ch<u>and</u>eliers
3. <u>Dash</u>board
4. St<u>atue</u> of Liberty
5. <u>Star</u>-Spangled Banner
6. <u>Triangle</u>
7. <u>Square</u> dances
8. <u>Plush</u> toys
9. Lieutenant <u>colonel</u>
10. <u>Comman</u>der-in-chief

ADD A LETTER (pg. 26)

O
O R
O R E
R O S E
S O R E S
S N O R E S
S E R M O N S
M O N S T E R S

SHAPE UP (pg. 74)

1. WHAT DO YOU CALL A FAT APE? A CHUNKY MONKEY.
2. WHY ARE CARDS LIKE WOLVES? THEY'RE PART OF A PACK.
3. WHAT DOES A VAMPIRE TAKE FOR A COLD? COFFIN SYRUP.

SCRAMBLED GO-TOGETHERS (pg. 27)

1. COMB and BRUSH
2. HAMMER and NAIL
3. NEEDLE and THREAD
4. PAIL and SHOVEL
5. CUP and SAUCER
6. PAPER and PENCIL
7. KNIFE and FORK
8. BOW and ARROW

FORTUNE COOKIES (pg. 24)

WHAT'S THE FASTEST WAY TO DOUBLE YOUR MONEY?
FOLD IT IN HALF.
HOW MUCH MONEY DOES A SKUNK HAVE?
ONE SCENT.
WHERE DO COMPUTERS KEEP THEIR MONEY?
IN MEMORY BANKS.
WHY DON'T COWS HAVE MONEY?
BECAUSE THE FARMER MILKS THEM DRY.

HELP WANTED (pg. 58)

1 – E	5 – H
2 – G	6 – D
3 – B	7 – C
4 – A	8 – F

DRIVING HAZARD (pg. 66)

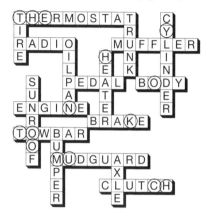

Answer: They honk too much.

STINGER (pg. 21)

GYMN**A**SIUM
EVER**Y**BODY
WEDN**E**SDAY
GENT**L**EMAN
BRILL**I**ANT
MICR**O**WAVE
STOP**W**ATCH
OVER**J**OYED
ENCH**A**NTED
ADJE**C**TIVE
STOC**K**ROOM
EXTRE**M**ELY
QUAR**T**ERLY
Answer: A Yellow Jacket

PICTURE RIDDLE (pg. 28)

A. EYES
B. BELL
C. STAMP
D. BOTTLE
E. CHERRY
F. HOUSE
G. SHEEP
H. TENT

Answer: They both rely on the batter.

DOUBLE-ACTING WORDS
(pg. 51)

1. EARTH
2. LIGHT
3. PLAY
4. RACKET
5. RAISE
6. KID
7. POOL
8. RARE
9. PAD
10. BLUE

DO-IT-YOURSELF (pg. 29)

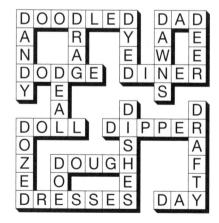

OUT OF SIGHT (pg. 30)

FOUR FITS (pg. 39)

1. HOSPITAL
2. CHAIRMAN
3. SEARCHED
4. GOVERNOR
5. HAUNTED
6. REMAINDER
7. CLASSROOM
8. BROADWAY
9. SPEARMINT
10. AUTHENTIC

TEE TIME (pg. 22)

1. Phoenix, Arizona
2. Chicago, Illinois
3. Dallas, Texas
4. Seattle, Washington
5. Baltimore, Maryland
6. Orlando, Florida
7. Lincoln, Nebraska
8. Honolulu, Hawaii
9. Fairbanks, Alaska
10. Denver, Colorado

IT'S NOT WHAT YOU SAY ... (pg. 72)

1. ARCTIC CIRCLE
2. BACKACHE
3. LONG DIVISION
4. LITTLE MISS MUFFET
5. SCRAMBLED EGGS
6. MOTHER-IN-LAW
7. LOW TECH
8. LEFTOVERS
9. HIGH FIVE
10. STEP ON IT!

DOUBLE TROUBLE (pg. 38)

BIRDS

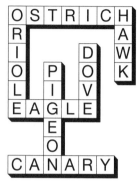

FISH

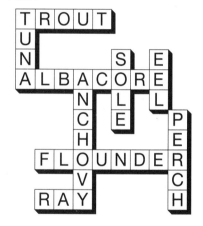

CHANGE OVER (pg. 84)

Answer: The weather.

BODY BUILDING PLUS (pg. 42)

1. BROWNIE	9. FIRE
2. THOUSANDS	10. RUSH
3. OYSTER	11. HEAL
4. SNEAKERS	12. HOT
5. LEATHER	13. LION
6. SENATOR	14. LANE
7. CHINESE	15. CLUE
8. SIMPLER	16. CRIB

AUTHOR! AUTHOR! (pg. 54)

Strays by Al E. Katz
Ouch! by A. King
The Guide to Beauty by May Cup
The Operator by Sir Gerry
Exotic Veggie by R. T. Choke
Musical Selections by Vy Olin
Betcha Can't Find Me!
   by Mr. E. Mann

DIZZY DEFINITIONS (pg. 65)

1 – F	6 – C
2 – D	7 – E
3 – H	8 – I
4 – J	9 – G
5 – B	10 – A

RIDDLE CROSSWORD (pg. 46)

L	I	K	E	S		I	N	K
O		I		A		C		E
W	E	T		N	I	E	C	E
		T		D				P
T	O	Y				Y	E	S
E				E		E		
E	N	T	E	R		A	G	O
T		R		I		R		W
H	A	Y		E	A	S	E	L

Answer: With a skeleton key.

JUSTICE IS SERVED (pg. 34)

1. JUNE
2. FREE
3. WADE
4. LATE
5. SODA
6. GROUCH
7. TOUCH
8. TOAD

Answer: Where does a judge eat lunch? At a food court.

NOT THE SAME OLD GRIND
(pg. 56)

What did the dentist see at the North Pole?

A molar bear.

INSTANT MESSANGING
(pg. 50)

1. SIMON
2. TIMED
3. IMAGE
4. DENIM
5. ESTIMATE
6. DECIMAL
7. GRIMACE
8. IMPORT
9. IMPRESS
10. IMPOSE
11. LIMIT
12. MIME

SUM SITUATION (pg. 8)

What did one math book say to the other math book?
Boy, do I have problems.

CLASSROOM CAPER
(pg. 60)

WATCH IT (pg. 48)

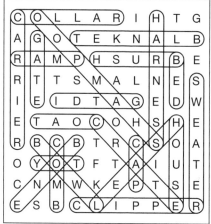

Answer: It gets a lot of ticks.

FACES IN THE CROWD (pg. 36)

A TRICKY SITUATION (pg. 55)

CUSHIONS	H	COUSINS
TROUBLES	O	BUTLERS
INVESTOR	T	VERSION
GREETING	G	INTEGER
EVIDENCE	N	DECEIVE
ORIGINAL	O	RAILING
DYNAMITE	D	ANYTIME
CIRCUSES	C	CRUISES
AWARDING	A	DRAWING
NUISANCE	U	CANINES

Answer: Touch and go

ANNA GRAM (pg. 52)

WELL-VERSED (pg. 63)
1. HOT/COLD
2. GOOD/BAD
3. THIN/FAT
4. MORE/LESS
5. LOVE/HATE
6. FAST/SLOW
7. NIGHT/DAY
8. LARGE/SMALL

FOOTBALL FUN (pg. 32)

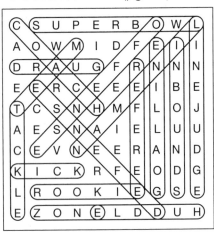

Answer: A wide receiver

BEFORE OR AFTER (pg. 78)
WHY ARE VAMPIRES UNPOPULAR?

BECAUSE THEY ARE A PAIN IN THE NECK.

WHAT LIVES IN THE WATER AND TAKES YOU ANYWHERE YOU WANT TO GO?

A TAXI CRAB.

CLEANING UP (pg. 68)
1. ADORABLE
2. GOALIE
3. UKULELE
4. VALUABLE
5. KARATE
6. OATMEAL
7. JELLY
8. BAWL
9. PUPPET
10. OCTOBER
11. RACE
12. TELLER
13. ZILCH
14. TYPE
15. LEOPARD

Leftover words:
At right heave I wing.
Answer:
It might leave a ring.

PUNNY WORDS (pg. 80)
1. GORILLA
2. ICON
3. LEAF
4. DISCARD
5. WATER
6. DESPAIR
7. TURNIP
8. DELIGHT
9. OLIVE
10. PECAN
11. POLICE
12. SPIDER

MEMORY QUIZ (pgs. 61–62)
1. Eight
2. The girl
3. Tulips
4. Checkers
5. Three
6. Taller one
7. Nothing
8. It is sunny.
9. Yes, two
10. Dalmatians

MISSING LINKS (pg. 70)

1. TEE <u>THE</u> IRS
2. COT <u>TON</u> GUE
3. DAM <u>AGE</u> NCY
4. CLO <u>SET</u> TLE
5. MUF <u>FIN</u> ISH
6. SUD <u>DEN</u> TAL
7. HAP <u>PEN</u> CIL
8. SPR <u>OUT</u> FIT
9. FAS <u>TEN</u> DER
10. INF <u>ANT</u> LER
11. VIO <u>LET</u> TER
12. BOB <u>CAT</u> NAP

BEAUTY TREATMENT

(pg. 53)

Answer: They use "hare" brushes.

SQUISH/SQUASH (pg. 44)

1. COUSIN/GRANDFATHER
2. MARCH/NOVEMBER
3. SWISS/COTTAGE
4. PILOT/NURSE
5. SEVEN/THIRTY
6. ELEPHANT/WOLF
7. KITCHEN/BEDROOM
8. DIME/PENNY
9. ARCHERY/BOXING
10. DUTCH/ENGLISH

EXCUSES, EXCUSES (pg. 76)

1. MY <u>HAM</u>STER CHE<u>WED</u> IT.
2. I <u>JUMPED</u> IN<u>TO</u> A LAKE TO RE<u>SCUE</u> MY FRI<u>END</u>, AND MY <u>HOME</u>WORK <u>DROWNED</u>.
3. A <u>HUGE</u> GUST OF <u>WIND</u> BLEW IT OUT OF MY H<u>ANDS</u> WH<u>ILE</u> WE <u>WERE</u> DRIVING MY GRAND<u>PARENTS</u> TO THE AIR<u>PORT</u>.
4. MY <u>FATHER</u> ACCI<u>DENT</u>ALLY PUT IT IN HIS BRIE<u>FCASE</u> W<u>HEN</u> HE WENT ON A <u>BUS</u>INESS T<u>RIP</u>.
5. MY <u>MOTHER</u> SPILLED <u>COFFEE</u> ALL OVER IT.

IF THE SHOE FITS (pg. 40)

ENCYCLOPEDIA WORDS (pg. 82)

FLOWER BED (pg. 64)

Answer: Chrysanthemum

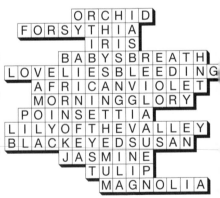